To all of my friends and family who helped us along the way and made sure we made it through this journey.
Each of you is so appreciated.
And to Scotty for showing me the way.
There is always a way.

Copyright© 2010 Jennifer Fura
Illustrations by:
Samantha Smith and Matthew Ulrich

For more information, contact:
Jennifer Fura
Email Author at: scottys-way@hotmail.com

Library of Congress Control Number: 2009914207
ISBN 978-1-935268-36-9

Attention Organizations, buyers and educational institutions:

Quantity discounts are available on bulk purchases of this book for reselling, educational purposes, subscription incentives or fund raising. Please contact our Sales Department at 216-255-6756.

Halo
Publishing International
www.halopublishing.com

Printed in China

Have you ever wondered what it would be like if you had to learn to do something a brand new way? I never did, but one day I had to figure out different ways to do things from how I had done them before. And I have figured out so many things—I just have my own way of doing them now.

I am Scotty, and I can pretty much do anything! I play all kinds of sports, like soccer and baseball. I like to play with my friends and ride my bike outside. I like fishing and drawing. I just got a new motorcycle and it is so fun to ride. You might think none of that is unusual, but I do all of that and so many other things with only one arm. It's not always easy to do all these things, and my way may be a little different from how everyone else does them, but I just do things my way because it works for me.

Let me show you just a few of the things I have figured out how to do my way:

I get myself dressed every day. In the beginning, my mom and dad had to help me out, but I really wanted to learn to do it myself and soon enough I figured it out.

Putting on socks took a long time and a lot of practice. But after some experimenting, I got it! I put my big toe in first, then stretch the sock over the rest of my toes, and just pull it up over my heel.

In order to put on a shirt, I lay the shirt out on my bed. Then I pick up the back of the shirt and stick my head in and pull it over my back. Then I can put my arms in, well one full arm, anyway! My right arm is really small, about 6 inches long.

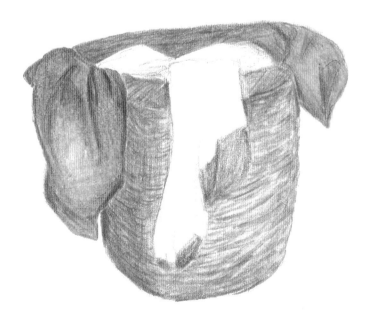

I can get myself ready each morning. In the shower, my shampoo and soap is in a dispenser that is attached to the wall. Most of the time I use my right elbow to push the button so the soap comes out.

Sometimes, I use my forehead! It's pretty easy actually. As with most things, it's different, but that's just my way. The toothpaste dispenser is a cinch. My toothpaste is already in the dispenser. I just push my toothbrush in there and the toothpaste comes out. I have all kinds of neat gadgets like this that help me do things by myself.

I can open all the doors in my house with one hand. This was especially important when I was little because my hand was so small. We used to have regular round door handles. My mom and dad took all of them off and replaced them with the lever type. Now, I can even open the door with my little arm if I have a messy hand without getting the handle dirty!

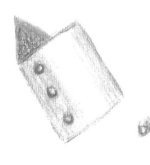

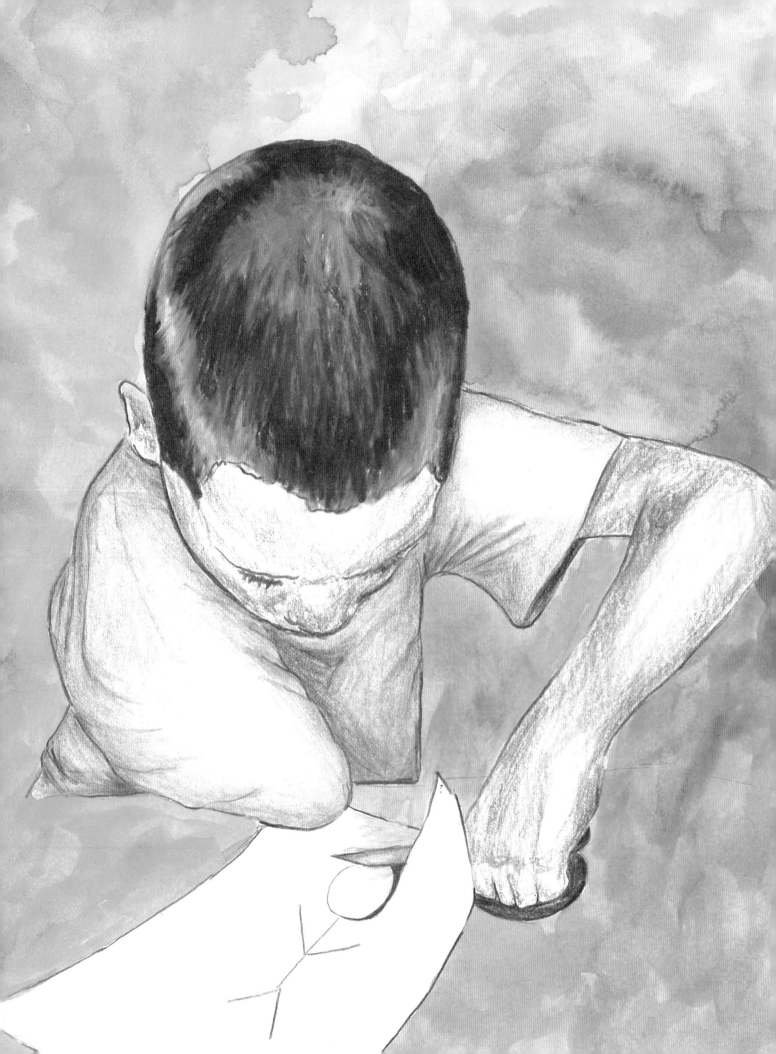

One of the hard things I had to figure out how to cut paper with scissors my own way. When I would cut a piece of paper, I didn't really have anything to hold the paper. What works for me is keeping the paper on the table and holding it down with my little arm. I have gotten pretty good at cutting out even small things. You have to do a LOT of cutting in first grade!

Speaking of first grade, there are a lot of new things everyone has to learn, but I had to learn my own way to do everything. One of those things was putting my chair up on my desk at the end of the day. My teacher, Mrs. Gauzza, showed us all how to safely tip over the chair then lift it up on the desk. I was a little nervous, but I wanted to try it. First, I flipped my chair over just like she said. Then, I used both my left hand and my little arm to squeeze and lift it up onto the table. All the kids cheered for me. I said 'Hooray!' when all my classmates started clapping. I felt pretty awesome! I was happy I did it.

There are so many things that you need a right hand for. When I want to take a picture, I try to prop the camera up on my little arm while holding the camera with my left hand. Then I can snap a picture with my index finger. Sometimes, I just take the picture upside down! That is my funny way!

Trying to stay balanced is something I am always working on. Trying to ride my bike without training wheels was scary for me at first. But one day I just took off. Now, my mom says I ride too fast!

I can even do headstands and pushups with one arm. It's tough, but I just keep practicing. It's especially hard to balance using only one arm!

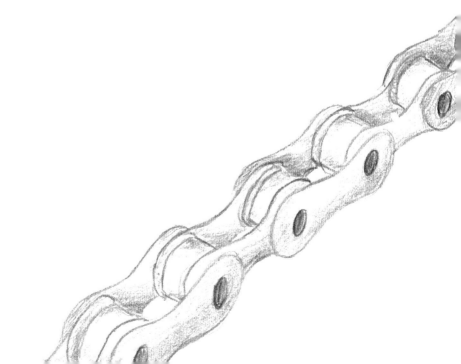

I love to play sports. Soccer is pretty simple because you don't need hands to play soccer! Well . . . maybe if you're throwing the ball or playing goalie. But even with one hand I do a pretty good job. I just figured out my way to do it.

My dad is really good at baseball. He has helped me figure out how to hold the bat to swing, how to hold my glove to catch the ball, and how to use my little arm to hold my glove while I throw the ball. This took a lot of practice. To catch the ball, I hold the glove on my hand while catching. Then, I quickly put the glove under my little arm so that frees up my hand to grab the ball and throw it. When I am ready to bat, I hold the end of the bat under my little arm. When the ball is coming, I let go with my little arm, then swing the bat back just a little with my left hand, and WHACK, there goes the ball! I am going to try football next!

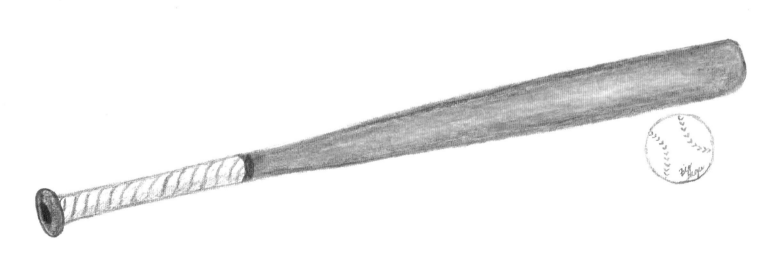

Fishing is so fun. My boat, Lefty, is named after me. I go out fishing on it all the time. I have learned to use my feet to hold the hook so I can put my worm on it. And I learned to use my legs to hold the pole when I catch a fish to reel it in.

I LOVE MOTORCYCLES! I have always loved anything with an engine. I like to ride electric cars, 4-wheelers, and tractors, too. But they are all made for right-handed people. The throttle is always on the right handle bar. Most of the time, there is a foot brake but sometimes it is on the left handle bar, which means I can't go anywhere! But we have figured out my way to do this, too. My dad moved the throttle to the left handlebar and then moved the brake so I can control it with my foot.

As you can imagine, there are just some things that I cannot do by myself. Or I'll be in a big hurry, or maybe even a little frustrated. I even have my own special way when it comes to this. My little sister, Carly, likes to help me. One time, I could not wait to go swimming, but I had to put my life vest on first. I was so excited that I just could not get the buckle together. My sister noticed I was having a hard time and she offered to help me. She clicked the buckle together and away we went. She is my fast way!

Now that I think about it, I really can do most everything with one hand. I can use my right little arm to help me with most of the things I need to do.

I can go apple picking and hold the bag with my little arm. I can go to the pumpkin patch and carry my own pumpkin away. I can swing on my swing set, climb a ladder, and even sharpen a stick to roast marshmallows. Actually, I need my dad when I do this because he has to watch me!

There are still many things I know I'll have to figure out as I grow up. How will I cook? What kind of job can I do? How will I water-ski or even fold my own laundry? Whatever comes along, I know one thing for sure: I WILL NEVER GIVE UP. I will always try, no matter what it is. I know I will just have to figure out my own way to do it.

After I read this book to Scott and reminded him of all the things that he had learned to do his way, he looked at me and said, "I love to be me!" After all he has been through; he loves the way he is. That made this whole project worth it, just to hear him say that. I believe he is teaching such an important lesson about acceptance and understanding. This can be proven by the way his classmates, and all the people he meets, treat him and love him. He has touched so many people with his kindness and smile. He is very independent, confident, and outgoing. I believe Scotty will be able to do anything he sets his mind to. I am amazed at the things he never thinks twice about. This book is a gift to him and a reminder to my family about just how far we have come.